DR. ZED'S DAZZLING BOOK OF SCIENCE ACTIVITIES

WRITTEN BY GORDON PENROSE

DESIGNED + ILLUSTRATED BY LINDA BUCHOLTZ - ROSS

©Greey de Pencier Books, 1982.
Books from OWL are published in Canada by
Greey de Pencier Books, 56 The Esplanade, Suite 306,
Toronto, Ontario M5E 1A7.

OWL is a trademark of the Young Naturalist Foundation.
*trademarks of the Young Naturalist Foundation.

Published simultaneously in the United States in 1993 by Firefly Books
(U.S.) Inc., P.O. Box 1338, Ellicott Station, Buffalo, NY 14205

Printed in Hong Kong

*Dr. Zed appears as a regular feature in OWL, the
discovery magazine for children 8 and over. For
subscription information write: OWL, 56 The Esplanade,
Suite 306, Toronto, Ontario M5E 1A7

F G H I

Canadian Cataloguing in Publication Data

Penrose, Gordon, (date)
    Dr. Zed's dazzling book of science activities

ISBN 0-919872-78-6

1. Science – Juvenile literature. 2. Creative activities and seat work
– Juvenile literature. I. Bucholtz-Ross, Linda, (date) II. Title.

Q163.P46   j502   C82-095012-2

CONTENTS!

You'll need:
about 150 mL (approximately 2/3 cup) dishwashing
  detergent (Joy works best)
1 litre (4 cups) water
a flat container at least 30 cm x 30 cm x 8 cm
  (12 inches x 12 inches x 3½ inches) deep
two plastic drinking straws
80 cm (32 inches) of string

Making the Bubble Frame
1. Thread the string through both straws. (It's easy if you
suck it through.)
2. Knot the string and trim off the ends of the knot. Pull
the straws apart to make the frame.

Making Rainbows
1. In the container, gently mix together the water and
detergent. Don't make it too frothy.
2. Holding the middle of each straw, dip the frame into
the soap solution. Lift it out slowly so that you don't burst
the soap film.
3. Tilt the frame until you can see mixed-up colours in
the film.
4. Hold the frame steady and the colours will settle into
rainbow stripes.

Make giant rainbow bubbles
Carefully wave your bubble frame with the soap
film in it through the air and up over your head.
Then move the straws closer together and a
huge bubble will take flight.

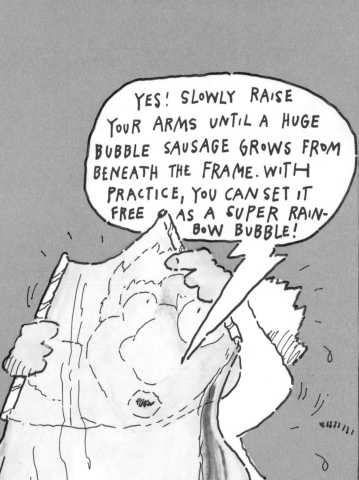

Special thanks to Dr. L. Kuhn

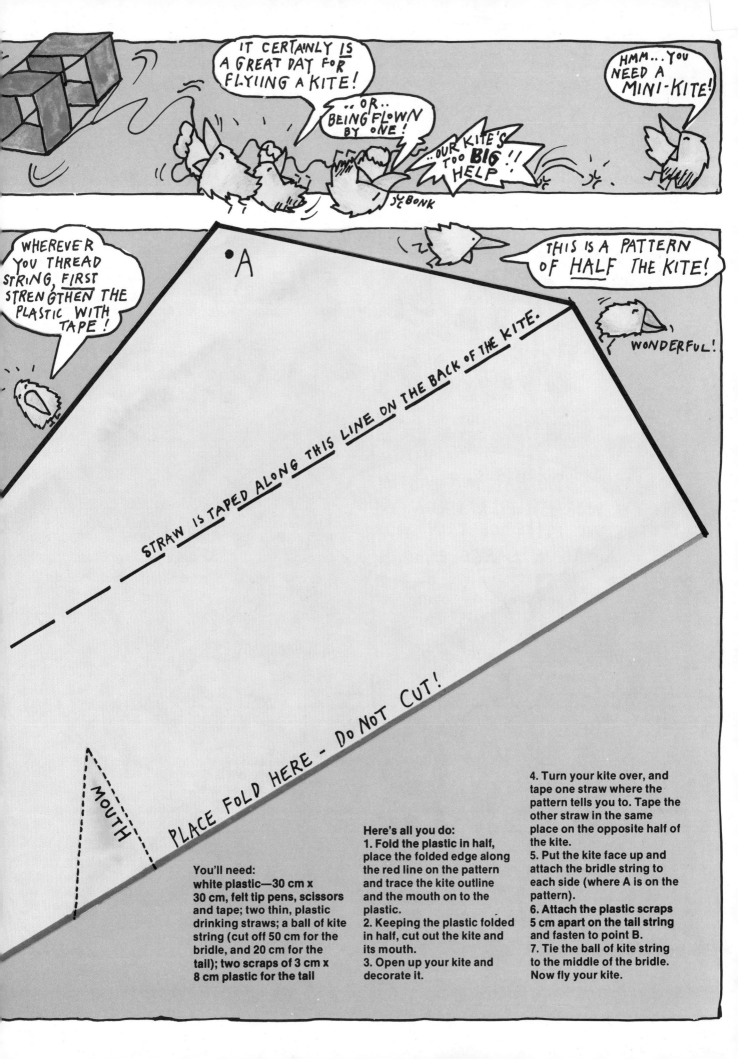

You'll need:
white plastic—30 cm x 30 cm, felt tip pens, scissors and tape; two thin, plastic drinking straws; a ball of kite string (cut off 50 cm for the bridle, and 20 cm for the tail); two scraps of 3 cm x 8 cm plastic for the tail

Here's all you do:
1. Fold the plastic in half, place the folded edge along the red line on the pattern and trace the kite outline and the mouth on to the plastic.
2. Keeping the plastic folded in half, cut out the kite and its mouth.
3. Open up your kite and decorate it.
4. Turn your kite over, and tape one straw where the pattern tells you to. Tape the other straw in the same place on the opposite half of the kite.
5. Put the kite face up and attach the bridle string to each side (where A is on the pattern).
6. Attach the plastic scraps 5 cm apart on the tail string and fasten to point B.
7. Tie the ball of kite string to the middle of the bridle. Now fly your kite.

You'll need:
a large, wide-mouthed glass jar
equal amounts of damp (not wet) soil and sand
worm food: leafy vegetables, grass cuttings,
  potato peelings and small amounts of coffee
  grounds
a piece of nylon stocking and an elastic band
a good memory so you don't forget to look after
  your worms

1. Fill your jar three-quarters full with layers of
sand and soil, as shown. Pack it all down very
firmly.
2. Put two to four worms on the soil mixture.
3. Sprinkle little bits of worm food on top.
4. Stretch the nylon stocking over the mouth of
the jar and hold it in place with the elastic band.
5. Put the jar in a cool, dark closet. Apart from
feeding and watering, do not disturb your
worms for at least a week so that they'll settle
into their new home.

You'll need:
a 30-cm piece of wire coathanger
pliers to bend the wire
a heavy steel bolt or lump of plasticine
a cork
two flat-headed nails
a pipe cleaner
a feather

To Make Your Noddy Bird
1. Bend the wire into a curve, as shown. Make a hook at one end and slip on the bolt or lump of plasticine.
2. Push the two nails (the legs) into the cork so that they're farther apart at the feet than at the body.
3. Make a head out of the pipe cleaner and fasten it around the narrow end of the cork.
4. Push the straight end of the wire into the flat, wide end of the cork. Stick the feather in just above it.
5. Find a shelf or table with space underneath, stand your Noddy Bird on it and give it a push.

You will need:
a small soup can with one end removed
a hammer
a nail
aluminum foil 4 cm x 4 cm
sticky tape
a large needle
thin cardboard 25 cm x 25 cm
a wax paper circle 10 cm in diameter
an elastic band
a cardboard circle 10 cm in diameter

Making your magic scope lens
1. Hammer a nail hole in the bottom of the can, as close to the centre as possible.
2. Tape aluminum foil over the nail hole.
3. Make a pinhole "lens" by punching a needle through the foil over the nail hole from the outside of the can.

Making your magic scope zoom tube
1. Roll and tape the cardboard square into a tube that fits snugly inside the can. N.B. It should slide in and out easily.
2. Tape the wax paper circle over one end of the tube, making sure the paper is wrinkle-free.
3. Cut an eye hole (about 2 cm in diameter) in the middle of the cardboard circle then tape the circle over the other end of the tube.

You'll need:
two 1.5 volt batteries out of your flashlight
masking tape
elastic band
a 3 volt bulb, bulb holder and screws (you can get them at a hardware store for about $1.90)

screwdriver
a scrap of wood 30 cm x 15 cm x 8 cm
scissors
thin, plastic-covered bell wire, untwisted to a single strand, about 2 m long
sharp knife

1. Tape the batteries together, positive to negative. Keep them pressed together with an elastic band. Screw the bulb holder onto the wood, then tape down the batteries, as shown.

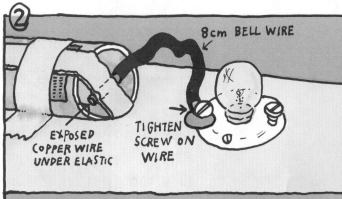

2. Cut two 8 cm pieces of bell wire. Using a sharp knife, strip off 1.5 cm of plastic from each end. Connect one wire as shown. Connect one end of the other wire to the opposite end of the battery.

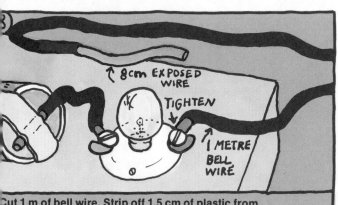

3. Cut 1 m of bell wire. Strip off 1.5 cm of plastic from one end and connect this end to the other side of the bulb holder, as shown. Strip 8 cm of plastic off the other end.

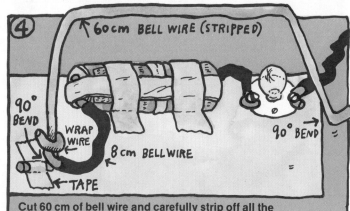

4. Cut 60 cm of bell wire and carefully strip off all the plastic. Tape one end onto the board and connect the free end of the 8 cm piece of wire from the battery to it, as shown.

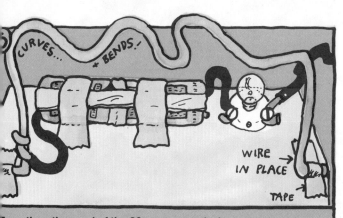

5. Tape the other end of the 60 cm exposed wire onto the opposite end of the board. When it's firmly in place, bend it into curves.

6. Finally, bend the exposed 8 cm of wire from the 1 m length into a loop. Before closing the loop, thread it over the curved wire.

You'll need:
a pencil
a piece of white card, 12 cm × 12 cm
scissors
red paint or felt tip pen
an empty, plastic toothbrush container with one
    end open
string or tape
a tablespoon
sugar
warm water
a cup
a small stick or twig

1. Draw a large flower on the card, cut it out and paint both sides *bright* red.
2. Stand the open end of the toothbrush container on the middle of the flower and draw around it. Cut out the shape you've drawn.
3. Slide the flower over the container and tape it in place about 1 cm from the open end.
4. Tie or tape the feeder to the small stick and push the stick into a flowerbed.
5. Make up enough sugar-water solution to fill the feeder. (Use one part sugar for every three parts warm water and stir well.)
6. Pour the sugar solution into the feeder. Check the level every few days and refill when it's half empty.

You'll need:
2 straightened-out wire coat hangers
garden tools or old spoons
seeds (beans, radishes or lettuce work well)
a sheet of heavy plastic (the type you buy at
    hardware or garden supply stores works best) at
    least twice as big as the area you are planting
needle and thread
bricks or heavy stones

1. Put the two coat hangers side by side and bend each into a large U-shaped hoop.
2. Find an open, sunny spot in the garden where the ground is soft. Prepare the soil for planting.
3. Stick the hoops firmly into the ground, one at each end of the seed patch.
4. Sow your seeds between the hoops, following the instructions on the packages.
5. Drape the plastic evenly over the hoops to make a tent. Make sure it doesn't sag in the middle.
6. Sew the plastic all the way around each hoop, as shown.
7. Use the bricks or stones to hold the plastic down on all four sides.

A MAGNET ATTRACTS THINGS. A MAGNET MAY [ATTRACT] A PIECE OF METAL [OR] EVEN THE RUBBER [ON] YOUR REFRIGERATOR DOOR!!

I JUST LOVE RACING BOATS!

ZAP!

WE'LL STICK AROUND!

You'll need:
a magnet - any shape that's easy to hold
a 5 cm piece of pencil
thumbtacks
permament ink felt-tip marker

three corks
masking tape
a plastic dishpan
water

BOW
STERN
2cm
THUMBTACKS
1cm

CORK
TAPE -STICKY SIDE OUT-

Making your boat race
1. The 5 cm long pencil will be the boat. Sharpen one end to make a bow (front); the blunt end will be the stern (rear).
2. Stick two thumbtacks on one side of the pencil - 1 cm from the stern, 2 cm from the bow.
3. Write "S" (for start) on the top of one cork; "F" (for finish) on the second. Colour the third cork.
4. Make a loop out of a 5 cm piece of masking tape so that the sticky surface is facing out and fasten it to the bottom of one of the corks. Now do the same to the other two corks.
5. Stick the "S" cork on the bottom in one corner of your dishpan, the "F" cork in the corner diagonally opposite, and the colour-topped cork in the centre. Now you have a racing circuit.
6. Pour water to a depth of about 2 cm into the dishpan. Balance the pan carefully between two stable chairs the same height. Place your boat in the water, hold the magnet under the pan. As you move your magnet beneath the boat, the boat will move.

S

F

YOU CAN TRY SLALOM RACING USING MORE CORKS! TRY RACING TWO BOATS FOR EVEN MORE EXCITEMENT!

HMM.. I WONDER HOW DEEP THE WATER CAN BE, BEFORE THE BOATS ARE NO LONGER IN THE MAGNETIC FIELD!

HOW VERY ATTRACTIVE!

S

F

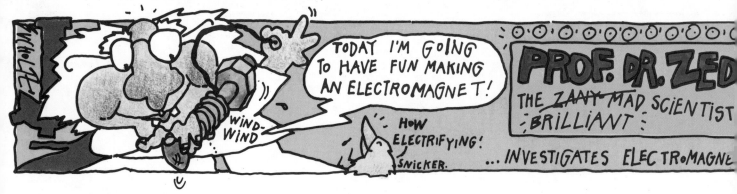

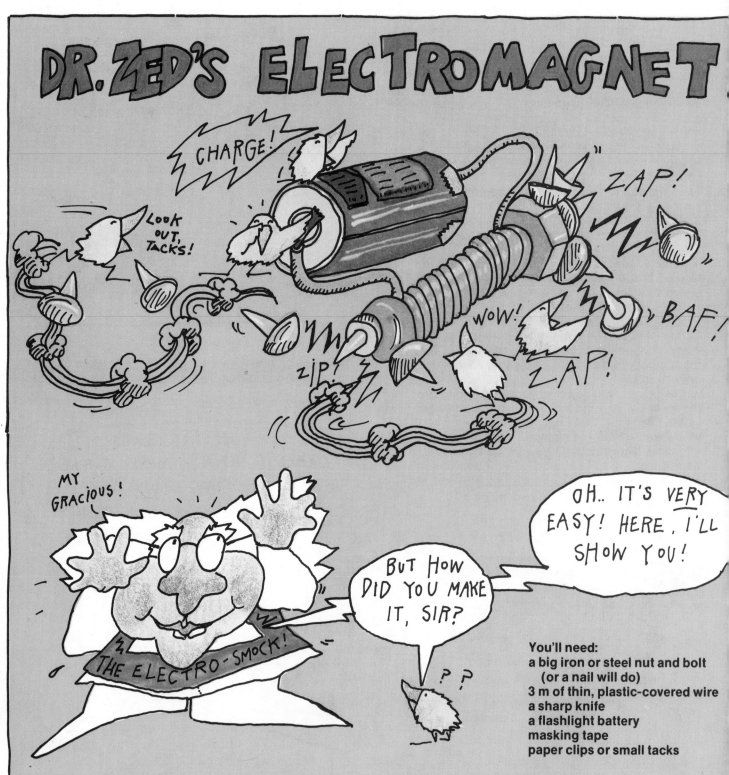

1. MAKING YOUR ELECTROMAGNET.

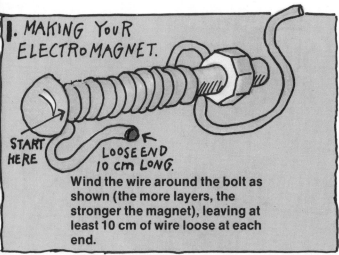

Wind the wire around the bolt as shown (the more layers, the stronger the magnet), leaving at least 10 cm of wire loose at each end.

2.

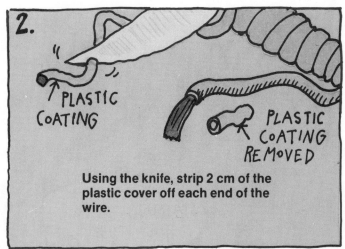

Using the knife, strip 2 cm of the plastic cover off each end of the wire.

3.

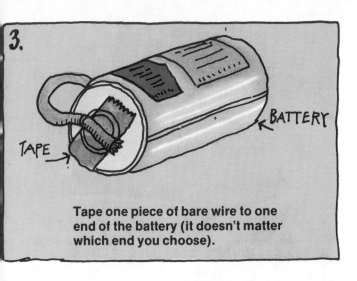

Tape one piece of bare wire to one end of the battery (it doesn't matter which end you choose).

4.

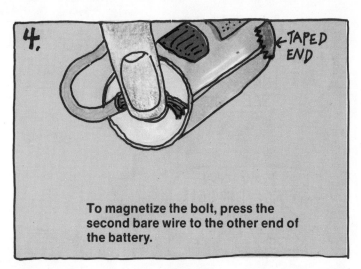

To magnetize the bolt, press the second bare wire to the other end of the battery.

You'll need:
a large, empty box for aluminum foil or plastic wrap
with the cutting edge removed
tape
a ruler
a pencil
a sharp knife
two pocket mirrors with
smooth edges (or tape the edges)

Preparing the Box
1. Tape the box shut.
2. Draw a square at one end of the box as shown.
Draw a line down one side of the box from B to C.
3. Turn the box over and do the same on the opposite end.

Fig. 1

Making the Mirror Slots
1. Carefully push a sharp knife into the box at A and cut from A to B.
2. Cut along the line B—C.
3. Turn the box over and cut along these same lines on the opposite end.

Fig. 2

CUT THROUGH ONE THICKNESS ONLY.

45°   45°

Cutting the Viewing Holes
1. Place the box on a table as in figure 3 and cut a hole 2 cm x 2 cm as shown.
2. Turn the box over and do the same on the other side.

Fig. 3

ABOUT 2cm

Slotting in the Mirrors
Slide one mirror into each slot and tape in place, so that the shiny sides face each other.

Fig. 4

MIRROR   VIEWING HOLE 'B'
TAPE
VIEWING HOLE 'A'   MIRROR

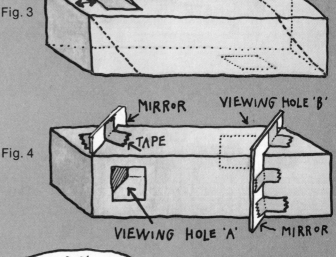

LIGHT RAYS COME IN HERE AND ARE BENT BY THE FIRST MIRROR!

LOOK HERE!

WHEN THE LIGHT RAYS HIT THE SECOND MIRROR THEY'RE BENT AGAIN AND COME OUT HERE!

For lots of information on volcanoes, see OWL magazine, April 1981.

You'll need:
a large, deep baking pan
an empty flower pot
a small, empty tuna can with one end removed
    plastic or paper cup with a top slightly wider
    than the can
scissors
masking tape
tinfoil
a teaspoon
white vinegar
powdered red or orange paint
baking soda

How to Make Your Mini-volcano
1. Stand the flower pot upside down in the middle of the pan.
2. Tape the empty tuna can, open end up, on top of the upturned flower pot.
3. Cut the bottom off the plastic cup and stand it, upside down, inside the can. To make it fit snugly, cut a V out of it and pull the sides together.
4. Cover the pot, can and cup completely with a large sheet of aluminum foil. Crinkle it so that it looks like a craggy mountainside. (If you want to make your volcano look more authentic, glue some soil to its sides or colour it with felt markers.)
5. Cut an X on top of the volcano and fold the foil down inside the cup to make a hole.

How to Make Your Volcano Erupt
1. Fill the tuna can with vinegar.
2. Add a heaping spoonful of red or orange powder paint to the vinegar.
3. Now add a heaping spoonful of baking soda to the vinegar. Mix and stand back.

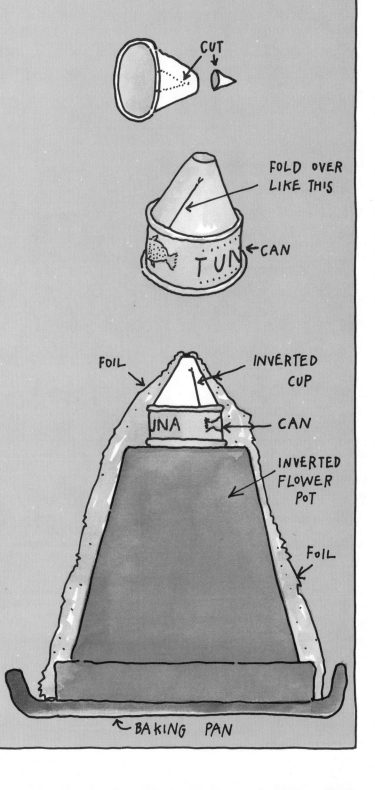

You'll need:
a large, clean plastic bottle with a cap (a bottle for car windshield cleaner works well)
a sharp knife or blade
a sheet of clear plastic or cellophane
a large spoon
tiny plants (weeds will do)
small, clean pebbles
barbecue charcoal
potting soil
water
masking tape

Making your terrarium
1. Using the sharp knife, cut two large rectangular holes on opposite sides of the bottle (ask an adult to help).
2. Cut two rectangles slightly larger than the holes out of the plastic or cellophane. Set these aside.

Planting your terrarium
1. Line the bottom of your terrarium with pebbles.
2. Smash a couple of charcoal briquettes (to do this, put them inside a paper bag and hit it with a hammer) and sprinkle the pieces on top of the pebbles. (Charcoal absorbs any odours caused by plants that might die and rot.)
3. Add 2 cm of potting soil to the terrarium and carefully water until it sticks together when you pinch it.
4. Ask permission first, then carefully spoon up a few small plants, leaving some soil around their roots.
5. Now poke some holes in the soil with your fingers and put in the plants, pressing the soil firmly around their roots.

Sealing your terrarium
Tape the clear plastic over the holes in the side of the terrarium so that there are no air leaks. Screw the cap tightly onto the bottle and put the terrarium in a warm, sunny part of your room.

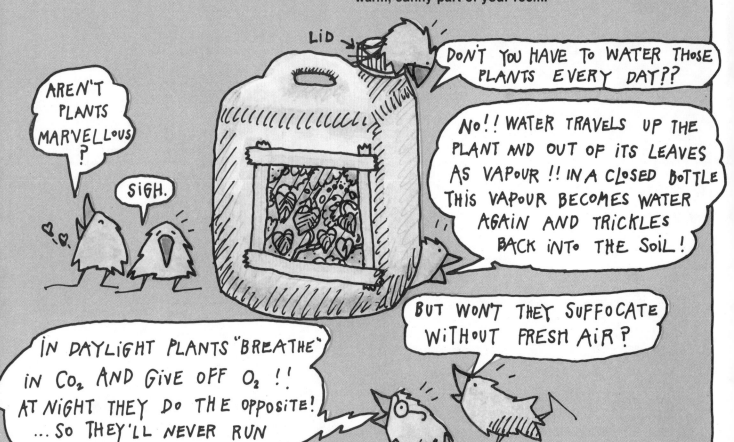

You'll need:
a piece of wood 35 cm high x 15 cm wide
a pencil and ruler
five 6 cm nails
a hammer
two pieces of string 30 cm long

a piece of string 40 cm long
a thin elastic band
an empty matchbox (the kind that holds wooden matches)
two empty cotton spools
plasticine

1.

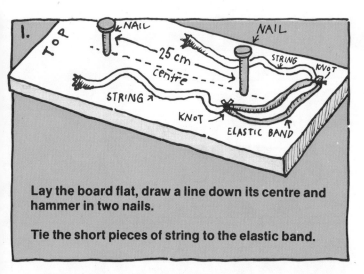

Lay the board flat, draw a line down its centre and hammer in two nails.

Tie the short pieces of string to the elastic band.

2.

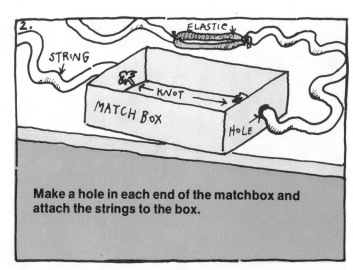

Make a hole in each end of the matchbox and attach the strings to the box.

3.

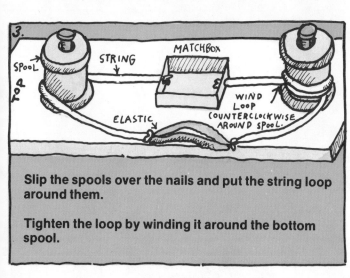

Slip the spools over the nails and put the string loop around them.

Tighten the loop by winding it around the bottom spool.

4.

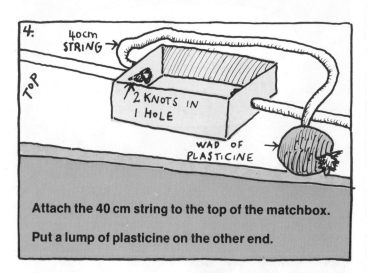

Attach the 40 cm string to the top of the matchbox.

Put a lump of plasticine on the other end.

5.

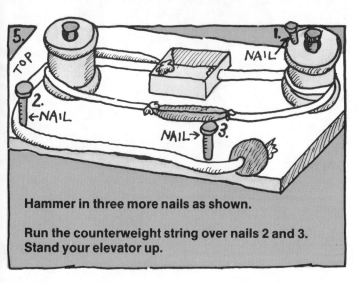

Hammer in three more nails as shown.

Run the counterweight string over nails 2 and 3. Stand your elevator up.

6.

You'll need:
hammer and a nail
a pill container at least 6 cm high by 4 cm in
    diameter, with a "lock"-type lid
two flexible drinking straws
scissors
a small piece of nylon stocking about 4 cm x
    8 cm
a twist tie
white glue

Making your insect catcher
1. Punch two holes 1 cm apart in the lid of the
pill container. Each hole should be the diameter
of a straw.
2. Put the short end of one of the straws in one
of the holes. If cut you cut the straw on an
angle it will be easier. Pull it through the lid
about 3 cm.
3. Double the piece of nylon to make a shape
about 4 cm square. Fasten it over the end of the
straw with a twist tie.
4. Pull the long end of the other straw through
the other hole in the lid. Extend it 5 cm into the
bottle.
5. The straws should fit very tightly into the lid.
Seal any gaps with white glue.

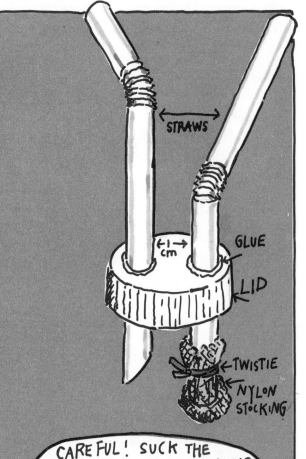

You'll need:
a thin drinking straw
a fat drinking straw (wide enough that the thin
 one can fit inside)
a stapler
sticky tape
stiff paper
scissors

1. Staple one end of the fat straw several times.
2. Seal it with sticky tape to make it airtight.
3. Fold the paper in half. Copy the diagram of
one wing and half the tail on one side of the
folded paper.
4. Leaving the paper folded, cut around the
edges of the wing and tail.
5. Make a rudder out of one thickness of paper.
6. Make the ailerons and elevators by cutting the
four lines as far as the stars, then fold the flaps
along the dotted lines.
7. Open the wings and tape them to the fat
straw, 4 cm from its closed end. Open the tail
and tape it to the same straw, 2 cm from its
open end, then tape the rudder to the top of the
tail.

To fly the plane:
Put the thin straw inside the fat straw. Put your
head back a little and, holding on to the thin
straw, blow into it.
Zoommmm!

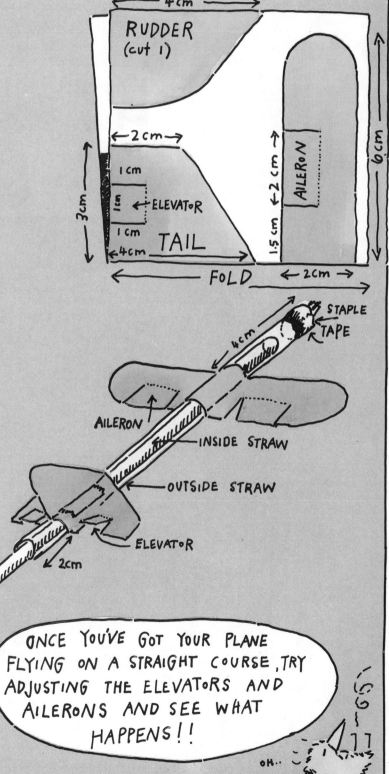

You'll need:
a cardboard box
a ruler
a pencil
a nail
a string
a knife, a fork, a teaspoon, a tablespoon

1. Place the cardboard box so that the open end is facing sideways.
2. Draw a line lengthwise down the centre of the bottom of the box. Mark four spots on it 5 cm apart. Make four small holes by pushing the nail through each spot.
3. Cut four pieces of string approximately 20 cm long.
4. Push each piece of string through a hole and knot each one inside the box.
5. Tie a teaspoon to the end of one piece of string, a knife to another, a tablespoon to another, and a fork to the last one.
6. Suspend the box between two chairs.
7. Tap the knife, fork and spoons with the ruler.

To make your own stethoscope you'll need:
a drill with 3 mm and 5 mm bits
an adult to help you drill a couple of holes
a hammer, small nail and scissors
a Marrette electrical connector, size 31 (from a
   hardware store, very inexpensive)
50 cm aquarium tubing
a concave-drawer knob about 5 cm in diameter
   (see diagram)
lid from a plastic margarine container

1. Drill a 3 mm hole through the top of the
Marrette connector (see illustration 1). Tap a
nail through the hole to remove the wire coil
inside. (The wire coil is not needed to make a
stethoscope).
2. Drill a hole 5 mm in diameter right through
the drawer knob.
3. Cut a disc slightly smaller than the surface of
the knob from the margarine top. Tape in place
around the edges.
4. Push the tubing into the knob so it touches
the plastic disc. Get ready to listen.

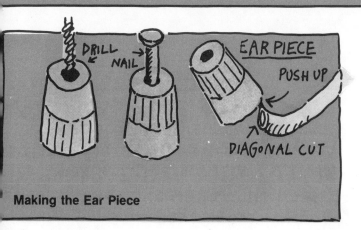

Making the Ear Piece

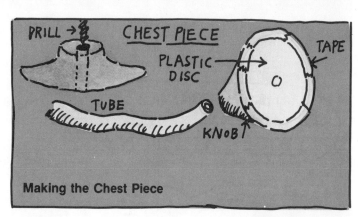

Making the Chest Piece

LOOK WHAT HE'S DOING WITH THOSE 2 MIRRORS!

PROF. DR. ZED
THE ZANY-MAD SCIENTIST
- BRILLIANT -
... HAS FUN WITH INCLINED MIRRORS!

PR ZED'S REFLECTING TWIRLING DISCO MACHINE !! *

WITH TWO MIRRORS YOU CAN SEE LOTS MORE THAN TWICE AS MUCH!!

WOW! ..WHY??

..SIMPLE! THE IMAGE THAT'S BEING REFLECTED IN EACH MIRROR IS, IN TURN, REFLECTED IN THE OPPOSITE MIRROR. PUT THE MIRRORS CLOSER TOGETHER AND YOU'LL SEE EVEN MORE IMAGES!!

ZED'S REFLECT-A-SMOCK!

← 90°

NEXT PAGE!

BUT WHERE'S THE DISCO?

You'll need:
stiff cardboard 15 cm x 15 cm (corrugated cardboard works best)
scissors
a pencil
a ruler

two pocket mirrors
masking tape
four straight pins
a tack
thin cardboard
a jar lid
felt-tip pens

60° ANGLE
(DRAW LONGER LINES)

1. Copy the 60° angle onto the corrugated cardboard. Now you have a base.
2. Tape the mirrors together on their non-shiny sides and stand them on the cardboard so they make a 60° angle. Hold their free ends in place with the straight pins (see illustration below).
3. Put a tack in the base where the mirrors join.
4. Using a jar lid as a guide, cut a thin cardboard disc. Mark its centre and decorate with patterns and shapes.

To put your Disco Machine together remove the mirrors and the tack from the cardboard, stick the tack through the centre of the disc and back into its hole in the cardboard. Put the mirrors in place and twirl the disc slowly. Cha-Cha Cha!

DISC

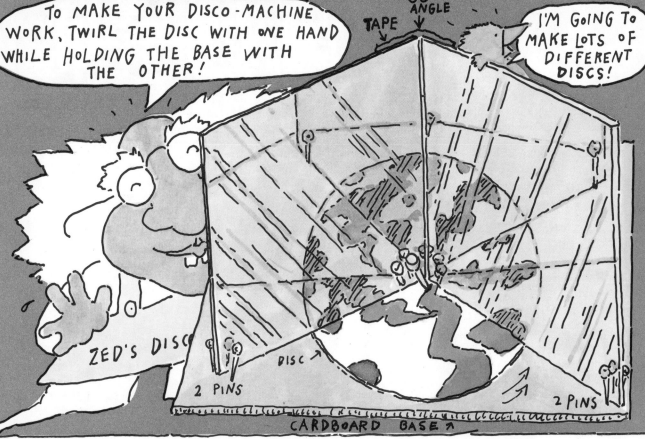

You'll need:

two 1.5-volt batteries
masking tape
an elastic band
three 2-metre-long pieces of thin, plastic-covered bell
  wire, untwisted to a single strand

a sharp knife
a 3-volt buzzer (you can buy one at a hardware, hobby
  or science shop for about $2)
a push button (hardware stores sell them for about
  $1.50)

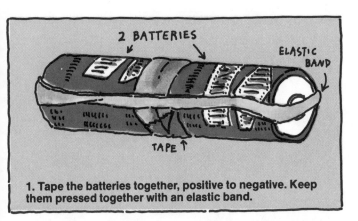

1. Tape the batteries together, positive to negative. Keep them pressed together with an elastic band.

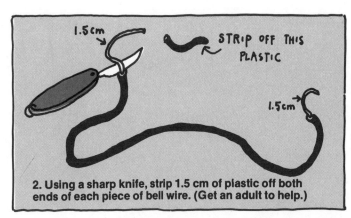

2. Using a sharp knife, strip 1.5 cm of plastic off both ends of each piece of bell wire. (Get an adult to help.)

3. Connect the batteries, push button and buzzer together like this:

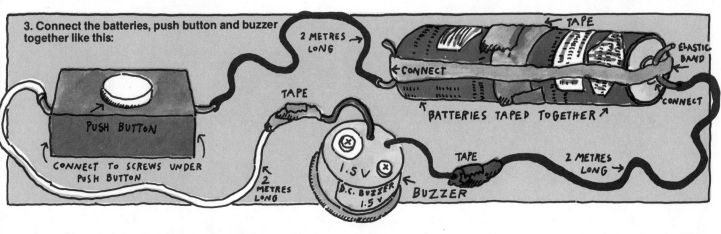

4. Tape the push button on the frame outside your door, and the buzzer and batteries inside. Make sure to tape the bell wire flat so that it doesn't get in the way when you open the door.

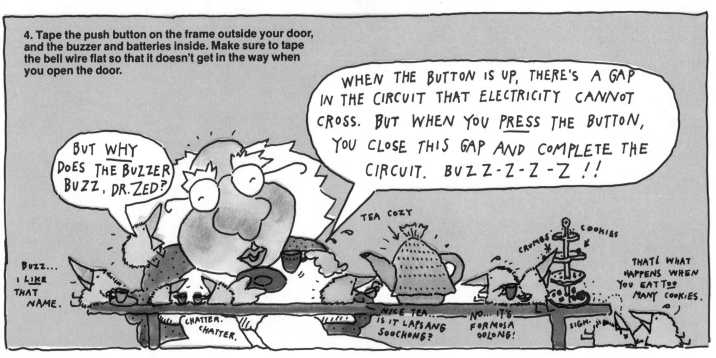

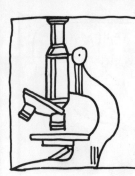

LOG:

... SCIENTIFIC, THAT IS !

HAVE YOU SEEN MY PENCIL?

?

DATE:	EXPERIMENT:	

NOTES:

AUTHOR'S NOTES

Learning can be fun. Out of this philosophy came Dr. Zed and his zany team of bird friends to introduce basic science concepts.

There is more to this book than just the jokes, however. The experiments themselves have been chosen because they're fun to do and because they reward readers with interesting products that can be used or demonstrated. In every case, the efforts of Dr. Zed's readers should yield fairly spectacular results.

It is our hope that most children using this book will be able to carry out all their experiments with minimum adult supervision. To ensure this, each experiment was tried by me with the assistance of children, then further tested by the children associated with OWL, Canada's magazine for 8 to 12 year olds, where Dr. Zed is a regular feature. Thus the book is designed for use in the home as well as in the classroom. All necessary materials, therefore, have been chosen for their accessibility, and we've stressed safety throughout.

Because we also feel it is important for children to discover things for themselves, almost every experiment encourages "experimentation". By making simple adjustments or following some of our suggestions for alternatives, users of Dr. Zed should be able to invent dramatic results of their very own.

Each experiment in Dr. Zed focuses on one major science understanding, and many touch on others as well. Because most readers are at Piaget's "concrete operations" stage we encourage them to "think" through the manipulation of real objects.

A careful balance of material for each of the various science disciplines has been maintained allowing readers to discover that explorations in all these areas are equally exciting.

DEDICATION

To my wife Marion and daughters Lynda, Donna and Sandra who shared their support for this venture,
To my friend Erle,
To all the people at OWL magazine for their challenges and encouragement,
To the children who showed me the joy to be found in experimenting with everyday things. It is with them that I share equally my portion of earnings from this book through charitable organizations who care for children around the world. — *Gordon Penrose*